STEAM JOBS IN

Wildlife

CONSERVATION

Emma Carlson Berne

WITHDRAWN

Rourke
Educational Media

rourkeeducationalmedia.com

Before Reading:

Building Academic Vocabulary and Background Knowledge

Before reading a book, it is important to tap into what your child or students already know about the topic. This will help them develop their vocabulary, increase their reading comprehension, and make connections across the curriculum.

1. *Look at the cover of the book. What will this book be about?*
2. *What do you already know about the topic?*
3. *Let's study the Table of Contents. What will you learn about in the book's chapters?*
4. *What would you like to learn about this topic? Do you think you might learn about it from this book? Why or why not?*
5. *Use a reading journal to write about your knowledge of this topic. Record what you already know about the topic and what you hope to learn about the topic.*
6. *Read the book.*
7. *In your reading journal, record what you learned about the topic and your response to the book.*
8. *After reading the book complete the activities below.*

Content Area Vocabulary
Read the list. What do these words mean?

biologist
data
ecosystems
habitats
populations
refuges
statistics
virtually

After Reading:

Comprehension and Extension Activity

After reading the book, work on the following questions with your child or students in order to check their level of reading comprehension and content mastery.

1. *What does a wildlife biologist do? (Summarize)*
2. *What topic might a wildlife educator discuss with a group of students? (Infer)*
3. *What does "banding" wildlife mean and why do biologists do it? (Asking Questions)*
4. *What area of wildlife conservation interests you the most and why? (Text to Self Connection)*
5. *Why is it important for people to work in wildlife conservation? (Asking Questions)*

Extension Activity

What is one way you can be a wildlife conservationist in your neighborhood or community? Look around and identify one type of wildlife you could help. Then write a plan to help that animal. Identify the problem you observe, then name the steps you could take to help solve that problem.

TABLE OF CONTENTS

The Big World of Wildlife Conservation 4
STEAM in Wildlife Conservation. 8
Research in Wildlife Conservation 26
A Day in the Life. 38
STEAM Job Facts. 44
Gossary 46
Index 47
Show What You Know 47
Websites to Visit 47
About the Author 48

THE BIG WORLD OF WILDLIFE CONSERVATION

A young woman crouches behind a fern, deep in the rainforest. She holds a clipboard as she quietly observes a group of orangutans. She counts the animals and records their behavior.

A man stands in front of a classroom. He points at a slide that shows how much of the world's forests have been destroyed. Students take notes as he lectures.

STEAM Spotlight

Wildlife Biology Goes to College

At the University of Montana, wildlife biology professors teach classes about Rocky Mountain flora, biology, and management of fishes, and ornithology, or the study of birds, among other topics. During classes, professors might teach students how to estimate wildlife **populations**—using dried beans instead of actual animals! They might also give students radio tracking devices and teach them to track each other around campus.

STEAM Spotlight

Studying Primates at Kibale National Park

Researchers working for the Kibale Chimpanzee Project in the Kibale National Park in Uganda spend hours each day observing chimpanzees—how they eat, hunt, and socialize. They write down what certain chimps do at certain times, each day. With this information, they can draw conclusions about chimp behavior. They can also study how humans evolved from primates.

A scientist stares at a computer. He has created a model of climate change. He is tracking what will happen to seabirds if ocean levels rise. Soon, he will write a paper about his findings.

STEAM Spotlight

Studying Seabirds

black-footed alb

In 2015, scientists working with the United States Geological Survey, the University of Hawaii, and the United States Fish and Wildlife Services published a research paper in a journal called PLOS One (Public Library of Science). The title of their paper was "How Will the Effects of Sea-Level Rise Create Ecological Traps for Pacific Island Seabirds?" The scientists studied what would happen to colonies of birds if ocean levels rose due to climate change. They found that if sea levels rise to a certain degree, the places where the seabirds live would become uninhabitable, to an extent. The scientists suggested that their findings show that people will need to make **habitats** for these birds in higher places where they will be safe from rising waters.

whooping crane

A woman leans over the edge of a motor boat. She lifts a thrashing water bird from the water and clips a band to its leg. Her assistant weighs the bird and notes its features. Then they let the bird go.

These people all work in the field of wildlife conservation. Wildlife conservationists have various jobs. But they all have a common goal: to protect Earth's plants, animals, and insects, and educate the public about their importance.

Why Band Birds?

Bird banding is an important tool for wildlife biologists. Scientists can use bands to track birds' migration patterns. Then, if a flock changes its migration pattern, scientists can try to figure out why.

The **data** collected from bird banding can also indicate how many birds are safe to hunt each year. If researchers find through studying banded birds that a species is at risk of becoming endangered, scientists can recommend ways to protect it. Or if a bird species' habitat has changed due to logging or construction, scientists can study the effects of the change.

STEAM IN WILDLIFE CONSERVATION

Virtually all areas of wildlife conservation require a strong foundation in STEAM education.

What does STEAM stand for?

Science
Technology
Engineering
Art
Math

Science

Conservationists may choose a specific field of science to specialize in. Or they may take a broader approach and combine several disciplines.

A **biologist** studies animals in their natural environment, from tiny microbes to humans, insects, reptiles, and mammals. Conservation biologists in particular work to protect endangered species by either altering or protecting their habitat. Conservation biologists also help to save or protect existing natural **ecosystems**.

STEAM Spotlight

sea otters

Otters, Kelp, and Urchins

Two scientists from the University of California-Santa Cruz compared data that measured how much kelp grew in a certain part of the Pacific Ocean. They also measured how many sea urchins and sea otters lived in the area. The scientists found that kelp forests grew better when sea otters were present—the otters ate the urchins and the urchins could not eat too much kelp. Kelp helps reduce atmospheric carbon, which contributes to climate change. The scientists concluded that protecting otter populations could be useful for reducing climate change.

kelp

sea urchin

Focus on Environmental Earth Science

Some people choose to focus on environmental Earth science as a career. An environmental Earth scientist would not just study wild animals and insects, but would also study physics, chemistry, soil science, biology, geology, and geography, just to name a few! This scientist would try to consider how all of these things affect each other and in turn, how they affect the planet's environment. They would especially focus on how humans are affecting Earth.

STEAM Spotlight

Fire Plan Forester Jamie Knight works for the Oregon Department of Forestry. She is the National Fire Plan Forester. Jamie often flies in small airplanes over Oregon forests. She tries to spot forest fires. When she does, she maps the fires using a GPS. She analyzes the smoke to understand how big the fire is. Then Jamie gives this information to fire managers. The fire managers use the date to decide how many firefighters to send, if any, and how much damage to structures the fires pose.

Forestry

Forestry is a more specific branch of biology. Forestry is the science of using and managing forests and using and managing the natural resources that come from forests. A forester might examine how much timber can be logged out of a forest without affecting a certain species of owl, for instance. Or they might study how much soil has eroded after a part of a forest has been logged.

This forester is climbing a giant sequoia tree. She will take leaf samples from the top of the tree to determine the water response to the California drought.

Ecology

When people study ecology, they are examining the relationship between living things—people, elephants, ladybugs, boa constrictors, maple trees, baobab trees, big bluestem grasses—and the environment of these living things. An ecologist might study how bacteria grow in a tank, or they might study how thousands of plant, insect, and animal species in one portion of a desert interact.

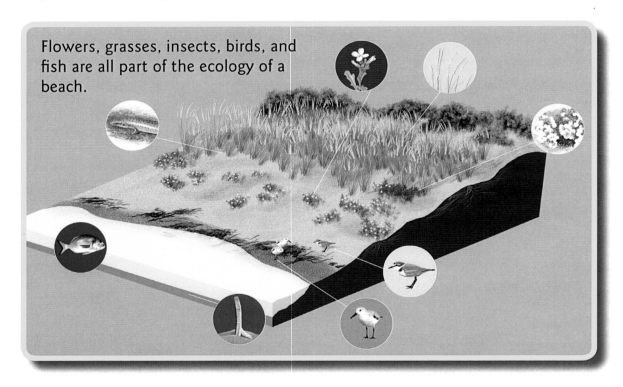

Flowers, grasses, insects, birds, and fish are all part of the ecology of a beach.

In the 1960s, ecologists showed that a big reason water in rivers and lakes was polluted was because runoff from certain ingredients in detergents and fertilizers was getting into the water. Cities and towns were able to change the way that water from people's homes and fields was fed into streams and lakes, so that the water was cleaner.

Dirty water pours from pipes into a body of water.

Ecologists also study how plants and animals might benefit humans. The Pacific Yew tree, for instance, makes a substance that is used in treating cancer—ecologists discovered this!

STEAM Fast Fact:

Biological oceanographers study how ocean wildlife reproduces, travels, distributes itself, and spreads.

Technology

Whether perched on a stool in a lab or crouching in a swamp, wildlife conservationists are constantly utilizing technology. In the lab, a researcher may build a model of a habitat on a computer, then manipulate it to see what would happen to a population of gorillas if a particular forest was destroyed.

Real STEAM Job: *Wildlife Biologist*

In the field, a wildlife biologist may chart a group of flamingos using a graph on a tablet computer, then compare that graph with others.

Some wildlife biologists use a technology called radiotelemetry to track animals. The wild animal is caught and fitted with a transmitter on a collar or another tiny device. The animal is let go. The transmitter sends a signal that's picked up by an antenna and transferred to a receiver.

identification number for tracking

BeetleCam

Up Close and Personal

Technology helps wildlife biologists get closer to animals in their natural habitat as well. Conservation photographer William Burrard-Lucas has created a remote control camera called the BeetleCam to take photos of wild animals without the intrusion of a photographer. The camera moves around on sturdy wheels, controlled from a distance by a photographer. A new computer technology has allowed researchers to listen to many bird calls at once and identify which species of birds are calling. Scientists hope to use it for other wildlife sounds, such as insect noises or even whales in the ocean. Biologists have even come up with a way to monitor whale health by gathering their—well, snot. Gathering blood from a whale can be distressing for the animal and hard for the researcher. Biologists can now use a small, remote-controlled helicopter that hovers over an area where whales are swimming. The helicopter has petri dishes strapped to the bottom. The whale comes up for air and blows out of its blowhole. Some mucus is contained in the spray and splatters the petri dishes. Voila! Sample collected!

Engineering

Engineers can work closely with wildlife as well. Conservation engineers design and build places for people to enjoy the outdoors while at the same time making sure that these places are safe for animals and not harmful to their environment. A conservation engineer might build a ski slope, an aquarium, or a zoo. They might help a national park decide where to build a new road.

In 2016, conservation engineers attending the annual Association of Conservation Engineers conference listened to

presenter Mark Russell from the USDA Forest Service describe how all-terrain vehicles (ATVs) were ruining the landscape at various points on trails. The engineers considered various solutions to the problem such as two different types of bridges, pipes laid under the trails, and ground coverings for the trails.

Engineering and Biology Together

Wildlife technology engineers use computer programs, remote-tracking devices, and other technology to help detect poaching of wild animals. Or engineers might work for government entities such as the U.S. Fish and Wildlife Service. These engineers might design dams that do not harm fish migration.

Engineers and biologists work together as well. Henry He is an engineer and a professor of engineering at the University of Missouri. He and his colleagues composed a portable system of cameras and sensors that can be placed out in an animal's natural habitat. The cameras "trap" animals' motions and record them. Then He designed a computer program to analyze the hundreds of thousands of photos that the cameras take over a period of weeks.

Art

Wildlife biology isn't only restricted to scientists and researchers. Artists and designers can examine and help the world of wild animals as well. Scientific illustrators are in high demand to draw detailed illustrations for science books and journals. Designers create digital animation for computer programs that can help scientists examine how animals move.

◀ The Bonneville Dam, located 145 river miles from the mouth of the Columbia River, included three locations of fishways. One on each end of the Spillway Dam and one at the Powerhouse on the Oregon side. Each fishway consisted of a collecting system, a fish ladder, and a pair of fish-locks. The fish ladders and fish-locks could be operated simultaneously or separately.

Real STEAM Job: *Wildlife photographer and videographer*

Wildlife photographers and videographers capture animals in their natural habitat and provide essential images to scientists. And scientific writers help take research and translate it into lively prose for press releases, policy papers, and articles for magazines and newspapers.

The Art of Wildlife Conservation

Dr. Kelvina Vulinec is an illustrator and a wildlife biologist. She teaches at Delaware State University and recently created a scientific coloring book for children. Children can color the images and learn about wildlife at the same time. Writer Nick Atkinson pens blog articles on wildlife on topics such as "What do deer eat?" and "What are antlers made of?" His writing helps the public understand wild animals better.

Wildlife photographer Marina Cano often shoots photos in Africa. In Amboseli National Park, she photographs elephants, a mother cheetah and two cubs, and giraffes at sunset. Her photos will show the public the beauty of these wild animals and perhaps convey how important it is that they be protected.

Amboseli National Park is one of the most-visited safari parks in Kenya. Its views of Mount Kilimanjaro and it abundant wildlife draw visitors from all over the world.

Amboseli National Park is famous for being the best place in Africa to get close views of free-ranging hippos and other wildlife species.

Math

And while wildlife conservation is all about animals, it is also all about numbers! Wildlife conservationists are constantly measuring groups of animals or insects, comparing those groups with others, comparing **statistics**, and examining charts, graphs, and tables—all math skills.

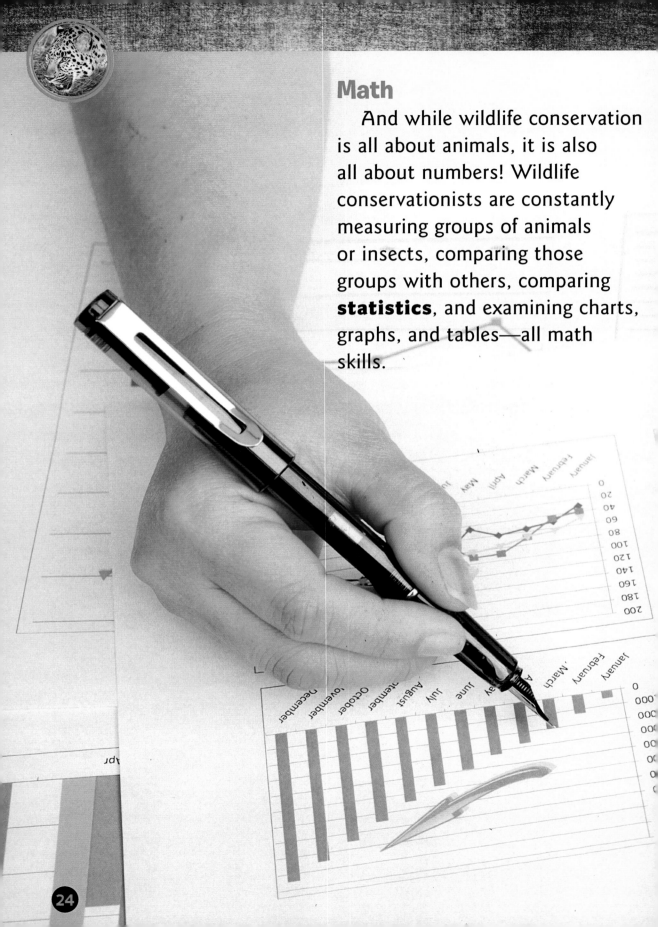

STEAM Spotlight

Working as a Wildlife Statistician

Dr. Emily Griffith is a statistician who often works on projects involving wildlife on land and in the ocean. She gathers and interprets numbers to assist biologists in their work. She has figured out how many fish live in a certain lake. She has analyzed patterns of sea grass on the ocean floor. She has examined the numbers of lake trout that return to their breeding grounds each year. Dr. Griffith is a teacher, as well. She teaches statistical classes for marine biologists.

RESEARCH IN WILDLIFE CONSERVATION

There are many paths to take when establishing a career in wildlife conservation. For those who prefer scientific study, whether in the field or in a lab, a job as a wildlife biologist technician might be a good fit. Wildlife biologist technicians go out into the physical area they are studying and gather information on plant and animal species in the area. They draw maps and write reports about what the habitat looks like.

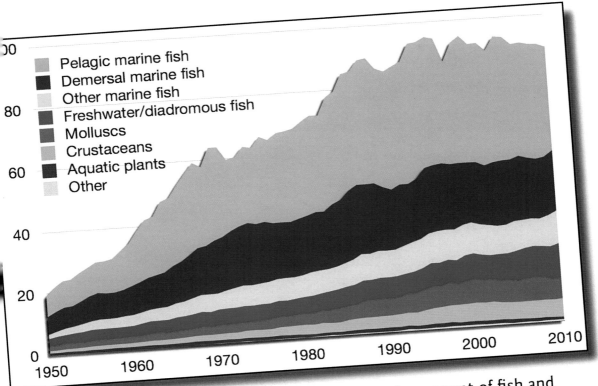

	Pelagic marine fish
	Demersal marine fish
	Other marine fish
	Freshwater/diadromous fish
	Molluscs
	Crustaceans
	Aquatic plants
	Other

This example of a computer-generated chart shows the amount of fish and other oceanic life over six decades. A conservationist might examine this chart to predict how much a certain species may decline over time.

A resource analyst for fisheries monitors, researches, and analyzes fish populations that live in fisheries and parks that are run by the government. A habitat technician studies how much vegetation and prey certain animals are eating and then enters that data into a computer in a lab. This research helps to create a model that would track how an animal population would survive if a certain food type were taken away.

Varied Careers

Working in habitat restoration would involve removing invasive plants and animals from a certain habitat. This person would also monitor and record the growth of native plant and animal species and educate local farmers and others in the area about why habitat restoration is important.

Wildlife rehabilitators prepare to release a loggerhead turtle after treating it for malnutrition.

This baby giraffe drinks from a bottle held by a wildlife rehabilitator.

A wildlife rehabilitator requires serious hands-on work. This job involves nursing injured or orphaned wild animals of all types back to health or independence, then releasing the animals back into their wild habitat.

Real STEAM Job: *Wildlife Conservation Marketer*

A wildlife conservation marketer works with wildlife groups to promote those groups to the public. The marketer is in charge of communicating the group's message to others outside the group.

Jobs and More Jobs

Park rangers patrol local, state, and national parks on foot, in ATVs, trucks, and on horseback. Rangers make sure people do not break park rules. They help stranded or injured people and wildlife. They also teach classes in the parks about wildlife and plant life and organize park exhibits about the natural world.

Real STEAM Job: *Wildlife Policy Analyst*

A wildlife policy analyst works with both wildlife groups and governments to try to create and change laws so that wildlife is better protected. A wildlife policy analyst writes papers directed to governmental bodies explaining why certain laws should be created, abolished, or altered.

A park ranger monitors a Kemp's Ridley sea turtle's nest. He takes photos and documents information about the eggs.

Educators Working for Wildlife

Some conservationists work as educators, helping people understand the delicate balance of Earth's ecosystems, and the roles people, plants, and animals play in conserving that balance. Some work for government organizations, forming and enforcing laws that protect the planet.

Conservation educators may work with museums and universities to train primary and secondary teachers in teaching wildlife conservation. These teachers then go back to their classrooms and teach their students what they've learned.

STEAM Spotlight

Teaching Conservation

At the Waterfront Center in Oyster Bay, New York, wildlife and outdoor educators spend their time teaching children from kindergarten through high school about the natural world on land and in the ocean. Educators work both inside classrooms, showing specimens and helping children to identify different parts of plants or animal skeletons, and outside, where they might teach a lesson on different kinds of compost.

Nature's Police Officers

Federal and state wildlife officers enforce environmental laws. They patrol state and national wildlife **refuges** by foot, car, and boat.

A wildlife enforcement officer working for the National Park Service uses binoculars to observe birds of prey

Real STEAM Job: *Wildlife Enforcement Officer*

A wildlife officer's primary goal is to enforce the laws that protect wildlife, while also making sure that the people who use the refuges are safe. A wildlife officer can issue tickets, arrest people, and investigate suspicious incidents.

STEAM Fast Fact:

Protecting Wildlife, Helping People
An average day for a federal wildlife officer might include teaching children how to fish, stopping people for driving unsafely in a wildlife refuge, or helping wildlife biologists organize a survey of an elk population.

Working Together

People in their various conservation roles work both independently and together. If logging in a region is causing a drop in a species of mouse, biologists will note the issue and bring it to the attention of government organizations. Then the government can respond by passing laws that limit the logging.

At the same time, wildlife educators can teach logging companies about the effects of their activities. They can teach local people how to protect the mice. Wildlife enforcement officers would patrol the area, making sure no one violates the logging ban, further helping to protect the mice.

A DAY IN THE LIFE

One day, in Tillamook, Oregon, a group of wildlife biologists drove out to a remote area of the West Cascade mountain range. They were in search of northern spotted owls, a species that is declining.

The biologists planned to tag the owls—catch them and place small leg bands on them—so they could keep track of each bird. They brought a man with them who was a certified bird bander. And they brought a container of live mice—a favorite owl snack.

STEAM Spotlight

Being a Certified Bird Bander

Bird banding is a special job in wildlife conservation. A bird bander works with researchers studying individual birds and bird populations. This person is trained to trap and handle birds safely and correctly place leg bands without causing harm. A bird bander needs a permit from the federal government. Bird banders are usually very knowledgeable and can identify many species, as well as the age and gender of a bird.

northern spotted owl

The bird bander called to the owls by imitating male owl noises. Then the biologists lured the owls out with the mice, and caught them.

The biologists held the owls carefully, and put the leg bands on. They recorded each bird's weight and inspected the birds for health problems. They took careful notes on each bird. Then the biologists let the birds go. Eventually, they will catch the owls again, and use the bands to identify them.

Both in the forest and in their laboratory, these biologists must use careful scientific skills of observation, testing, and recording. They must know how to utilize technology to record and map the owl population.

The biologists compare statistics on each owl and make predictions about the health of the owls and their ecosystem—all essential STEAM skills, being applied in the real working world.

A wildlife biologist uses a pooter to collect specimens.

STEAM JOB FACTS

Wildlife Biologist

Important Skills: scientific reasoning, scientific problem-solving, data-gathering, analysis, computer and technological understanding

Important Knowledge: computers, mathematics, biology, ecology, forestry, animal science

College Major: wildlife biology, zoology, environmental science

Wildlife Conservation Marketer

Important Skills: writing, synthesizing information conveying information, communicating with different groups

Important Knowledge: English, writing, computers, public speaking

College Major: wildlife biology, environmental science, marketing, communications, English

Wildlife Educator

Important Skills: conveying information, synthesizing information, using visual aids, active listening, problem-solving

Important Knowledge: writing, biology and other sciences, computers, mathematics, public speaking

College Major: wildlife biology, zoology, environmental science

Wildlife Enforcement Officer

Important Skills: active listening, understanding human behavior, organizational skills, judgment and decision-making

Important Knowledge: psychology, human behavior, leadership

College Major: ecology, forestry and fisheries science, wildlife biology, criminal justice

Wildlife Policy Analyst

Important Skills: writing, synthesizing information, conveying information, computer skills, critical thinking

Important Knowledge: English, writing, computers, mathematics, public speaking

College major: wildlife biology, environmental science, zoology, ecology

Wildlife Photographer and Videographer

Important Skills: computer and technological understanding, visual design and understanding, judgment and decision-making,

Important Knowledge: photography, computers, design, camera technology

College major: wildlife biology, environmental science, photography, art and design

GLOSSARY

biologist (bye-AH-lug-jist) : a person who studies life and all living things

data (DAY-tuh): information collected in a place so that something can be done with it

ecosystems (EE-ko-sis-tuhms): all the living things in places and their relationship to their environment

habitats (HAB-i-tats): the places where animals or plants are usually found

populations (pahp-yuh-lay-shuns): the total number of people or animals that live in certain places

refuges (REF-yooj-ez): safe places for animals or people

statistics (stuh-TIS-tiks): facts or pieces of information taken from studies that cover a much larger quantity of information

virtually (VIR-choo-uh-lee): almost or nearly

INDEX

biologist 7, 9, 14, 15, 19, 22, 25, 26, 35, 36, 38, 40, 40

biology 4, 10, 11, 19

conservation 7, 8, 15, 16, 24, 26, 29, 32, 33, 36, 38

data 7, 9, 27

educator 32, 33, 37

federal wildlife officer 35

habitat 6, 7, 7, 14, 15, 19, 20, 26, 27, 28, 29

lab 14, 26, 27

math 8, 24

planet 32

science 6, 8, 10, 11, 19

technology 8, 14, 15, 19, 42

wildlife conservationists 7, 14, 24

SHOW WHAT YOU KNOW

1. Define wildlife conservation.
2. Name three jobs you can do if you are a wildlife conservationist.
3. Explain how a wildlife biologist uses technology in his or her job.
4. What skills would you need to become a federal wildlife officer or a wildlife law enforcement officer?
5. What is one activity a wildlife educator might do in his or her job?

WEBSITES TO VISIT

www.fws.gov/international/education-zone/conservation-kids.html

www.nwf.org/Kids.aspx

www.kids.sandiegozoo.org/conservation

ABOUT THE AUTHOR

Emma Carlson Berne has written over eighty books for children and young adults. She especially loves writing about sports, history, and the outdoors. When she's not writing books, Emma rides horses, runs after her three little boys, and walks in the woods near her home in Cincinnati, Ohio.

Meet The Author!
www.meetREMauthors.com

www.rourkeeducationalmedia.com

PHOTO CREDITS: Cover and title page background © maodoltee, orangutan © Sergey Uryadnikov, amur leopard (cover and page headers) © Warren Metcalf, hawksbill turtle © Brent Barnes; pages 4-5 orangutans © UDKOV ANDREY, chimpanzee © Przemyslaw Skibinski, teacher © Andrey_Popov; page 6 scientist © audiLab, 6a © bikeriderlondon, page 7 © vagabond54, page 8-9 microscope © Billion Photos, dinghy © Maksimilian, otters © MODpix, kelp © Brent Barnes, sea urchins © Shu Ba; page 10-11 inspecting wheat © Hadrian, water sample © Francescomoufotografo, giant sequoia © Candia Baxter, fire © emattil; page 13 © oa55, turtle © Polly Dawson; page 14 map © Olinchuk, leatherback © IrinaK, satellite © bluebay, man on laptop © Marjoli Pentz; page 16-17 aquarium © Tanachot Srijam, ATVs © Evgeny Starkov; page 18 © Rigucci; page 20-21 elephants © Sergey Novikov, arctic shot © starchaser, man in water © aaltair; page 23 map of Africa © Bardocz Peter; page 24-25 © kanchana_koyjai; page 26 © boonchoke, page 27 © page 28-29 turtle release © Thomas Barrat, squirrel © Adriana Margarita Larios Arellano, giraffe © Fiona Ayerst; page 30-31 © JB Manning, female ranger © LMspencer; page 32-33 © goodluz; page 36-37 © MARGRIT HIRSCH, page 38 bird banding © Maksimilian; All photos from Shutterstock. com except: page 12 © © Nicolas Fernandez | Dreamstime.com, page 22 map of park © Lencer   https://creativecommons.org/licenses/by-sa/3.0/deed.en , page 23 Mt Kilimanjaro © © Sergey Pesterev / Wikimedia Commons / CC BY-SA 4.0 , hippos © Graeme Shannon (Colorado State University) https://creativecommons.org/licenses/by/4.0/deed.en ; Epipelagic https://creativecommons.org/licenses/by-sa/3.0/deed.en ; page34-35 © raptor monitoring NPS/Andrew Kuhn, car © Daniel Schwen   https://creativecommons.org/licenses/by-sa/4.0/deed.en car and boat © NPS; pages 38-41 © NPS photos by Emily Brouwer https://creativecommons.org/licenses/by/2.0/deed.en; page 43 entomologist © © Gabriela Insuratelu | Dreamstime.com, woman with binoculars © Djtaylor | Dreamstime.com

Edited by: Keli Sipperley

Cover and Interior design by: Nicola Stratford   www.nicolastratford.com

Library of Congress PCN Data

STEAM Jobs in Wildlife Conservation / Emma Carlson Berne
(STEAM Jobs You'll Love)
ISBN 978-1-68342-396-6 (hard cover)
ISBN 978-1-68342-466-6 (soft cover)
ISBN 978-1-68342-562-5 (e-Book)
Library of Congress Control Number: 2017931287

Printed in the United States of America, North Manchester, Indiana